• MEET •
GEORGES SEURAT

Read With You
Center for Excellence in STEAM Education

Read With You

ISBN: 979-8-88618-297-2
First Edition December 2022

Circus Sideshow (Parade de Cirque), 1887–1888

The Lighthouse at Honfleur, 1886

Seascape at Port-en-Bessin, Normandy, 1888

Oil Sketch for "A Sunday on La Grande Jatte – 1884," 1884

A Sunday on La Grande Jatte – 1884, 1884-1886

The Watering Can – Garden at Le Raincy, 1883

La Maria, Honfleur, 1886

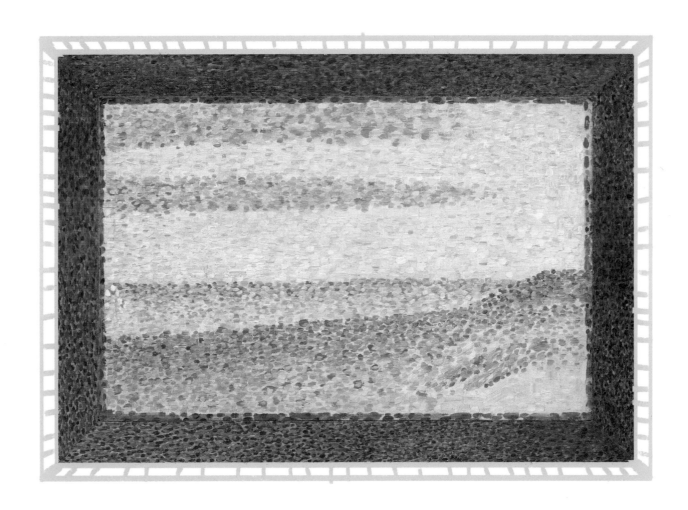

Seascape (Gravelines), 1890

Find Examples

This painting is *The Forest at Pontaubert* (1881).

Based on the light and color, what time of day do you think it is in this painting?

Compare this painting to *Seascape at Port-en-Bessin.* How are the greens different?

Where do you see dots most clearly in the painting?

Where did Seurat mix dots of distinct colors?

Do you see any longer strokes?

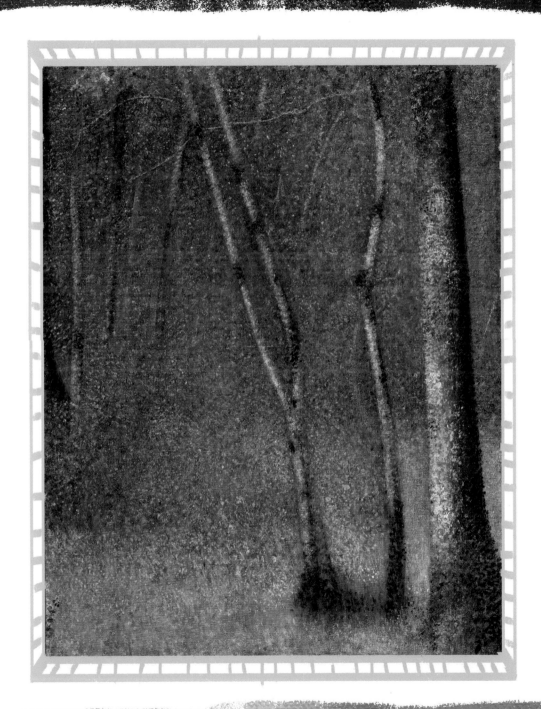

Connect

This lithograph is *Gray Weather, La Grande Jatte*, (c. 1886-1888)

How are the dots of the leaves different from the grass dots?

Can you find another painting in the book that shows the same place?

La Grande Jatte is an island in France. Based on the two paintings, would you like to visit? Why?

If you painted a place twice, once in the sunshine and once in gray weather, how would the pictures be different?

Craft

Option 1

1. Think of a place you want to draw and make three practice sketches with pencil.

2. Pick your favorite sketch.

3. Use markers to color in the sketch with dots. Press down gently, or the markers may break!

Option 2

1. Trace a picture that you like on a piece of white paper.

2. Look at the picture and find the darkest and lightest parts.

3. Fill in your drawing with pen dots close together for the darkest parts and spread-out pencil dots for the lightest parts!

Explore fun facts about interesting painters by visiting
https://www.readwithyou.com/pages/meet-the-artist-activities